MISADVENTURES IN MATURE DATING

AUDREY LINDT
JACQUELINE HAIGH

Copyright © 2018 by Audrey Lindt & Jacqueline Haigh

All rights reserved.

No part of this book may be reproduced in any form or by any electronic or mechanical means, including information storage and retrieval systems, without written permission from the author, except for the use of brief quotations in a book review.

FOREWORD

Are you ready for an adventure?

This was me: 60-plus, divorced from a difficult marriage and disillusioned with men overall. I had raised my two children who were now on their chosen paths and focusing on their own needs.

Through hard work and perseverance, I had achieved the career I wanted, which gave me a certain financial freedom and independence. Yet I still felt hollow inside. I had lost motivation for everything. Each day I asked myself, why am I waking up in the morning? What reason do I have to carry on? What is my purpose here on Earth?

Up until now, my life had been dedicated to my

everyday duties: work and children. I didn't have any free time so never had to worry about what to do with it. Everything was arranged according to my busy schedule, with never a moment to myself.

Then one day I didn't have to take anyone to school or to their friends for play time. I couldn't go on holiday with my children as they had their own plans. Yes, I had a good social life but, afterwards, I still went home alone. All the evening events I attended, I was with a female friend. Something was missing.

Finally, in the silence, I heard a small, still voice. It was my heart, still craving to experience the wonderful feelings that can exist between a woman and a man. For one more time in my life, I wanted to experience real love, a love based on honesty, trust and respect.

Night after night, I dreamt about this, but I still didn't do anything about it. Perhaps I was waiting for destiny to make its move. Then one day it did, in the form of my daughter who started me on this adventure, the one I share with you now. I hope you enjoy the ride.

ACKNOWLEDGMENTS

I would like to thank my beloved daughter, my best friend, who guided me onto this path, one I never thought that I would go on.

"Happiness depends upon ourselves"

Aristotle (384-322 BC)

ONE

TAKING THE PLUNGE

This is my story. I never expected to tell it and I don't yet know how it ends…

I turned sixty-one last birthday but, in my heart, I still feel thirty-five. A few months ago, I was in London visiting my daughter, Lana. She's a wonderful young woman of twenty-five, wise beyond her years, and we're the best of friends.

We were sitting in a café, chatting about nothing in particular, when she puts down her cappuccino and says that she has something to tell me. Of course, my mother's mind starts spinning. What has she done? Is she in trouble? Is she pregnant?

But then Lana reveals her guilty secret. She has registered me on an internet dating site. Me! She's opened the account, uploaded a photo and even written my profile. I can't believe that my own daughter has set me up like this. But I know she just wants to see me happy. I finally divorced her father three years ago, but our three decades together were not happy ones.

My ex-husband was constantly unfaithful yet, somehow, I couldn't leave. He had some hold over me. And, of course, there were excuses — so many. Some time ago, I was often travelling for work. I had a strong intuition that he was seeing someone, a woman with long hair, who was using my cosmetics when she stayed. But when I asked him, he denied it — how could I think such a thing?

So, the next time before I left, I set up a hidden camera in our bedroom. When I returned, I watched the video and there she was, in my bed, the woman with long hair. When I confronted my ex, he made the usual excuses and I never did show him the proof. I don't know why. Scared, I guess. I have never told Lana this story. He's her father after all. And, despite everything, he gave me my wonderful daughter, for which I will be forever grateful.

Throughout my life, to escape the problems in my marriage, I focused on my career instead. Thus, I became very successful in business, a CEO. I put my own emotional needs to one side and focused on giving my children the best life I could.

And now my daughter is here, taking a break from her glamorous job in London, to tell me that it's time for me to live the best life I can and find someone new. She shows me the website, an exclusive one to find eligible millionaires.

"You've worked hard to create a good standard of living, Mum," she declared. "Your partner should be on the same level."

She clicks through to my profile. It's strange to see yourself described by someone else, like a luxury product in a human catalogue.

But she's done well — I wish I felt like the person she describes! It's true that I take care of myself, eat healthfully and exercise, and look young for my age. But is it possible to meet Mr Right online? Can I really find love again? Or, perhaps it would be closer to the truth to say, for the first time...

Like most so-called "silver surfers," I struggle with

technology. I watch Lana, who is like a being from the future, as her fingers fly over her iPhone to show me more.

"Look, Mum," she exclaims. "Ten men have messaged you already!"

We scroll through their profiles; they seem attractive, wealthy, kind. They say that I look great. They love my smile. They would like to learn more about me. I can't reply because the one thing my daughter hasn't done, is paid. Well, that's what mums are for!

So, will I go for it? Lana asks me. Will I take the plunge?

TWO

FIRST CONTACT

"Life shrinks or expands in proportion to one's courage."

So said the French writer Anais Nin. I decided to go for it and joined the dating site for six months. Well, what did I have to lose? Only about £300, a small price to find love.

In the three years since my divorce, I hadn't been looking for anyone new. To be honest, marriage had left me with a low opinion of the unfair sex. I was disappointed with men and considered them, at best, stupid; at worst, cruel.

I had a good social life and lots of friends. I didn't need a lover. My passion was playing with different kinds of balls — little white ones on the golf course. Now, I reasoned, it was time for that to change. I didn't want to be alone forever. Yet, I was still too nervous to reply to the first message.

"You write it," I told Lana.

Like a cyber Cyrano De Bergerac, my brilliant daughter crafted the perfect reply, friendly yet brief, as if I was too busy with my fabulous life to say more.

And so it began. When I left London to go back home, I started to write back to my potential suitors myself. If someone contacted me, I would check their profile to see if they looked okay and then answer. I never approached men first. Maybe I'm too old-fashioned. Or just plain scared.

Being on the dating site got me thinking about how I wanted this next chapter of my life to be. I reduced my duties at work and decided to enjoy my time fully, creating the space for a potential relationship.

It all started so well. I received lots of messages from men about my own age or even a few years younger. They were clever, handsome, and rich. I could have kicked myself. Why had I been suffering for so many years when I was clearly a "hot woman" and there were so many interesting guys out there?

Their messages were full of love and promises straight away. I have to admit I was a little confused. I'd never experienced this before. I was twenty-five when I met my husband in a café in the capital of my home country, where the young people used to go. He came up to my table to buy me a coffee. It sounds so simple now, so innocent.

I wasn't that interested in him, but he was very kind to me. They always are at first. I gave him a chance and, later on, I fell in love. So deeply that I couldn't see what was really going on. My mother never liked him. Maybe mothers always know. But that was then. Now people don't meet in cafés or dances but in the virtual space — where no one can hear you scream.

The men that contacted me online came in waves. The first lot were divorced because their wives had cheated on them. I was surprised. These were good-looking guys; why did their wives play away?

These divorcés were angry. But, deep down, so was I. The second wave were widowers. They had lost the love of their lives after long and happy marriages but were hoping that lightening could strike twice.

Some had teenage children, some none. I explained that I didn't want to take responsibility for bringing up any more infants. It was time for me to enjoy myself.

"Don't worry," one man said. "They won't bother you. I have nannies."

"I promise to give you all my attention," cooed another. "Your life will be like a queen. No one has ever treated you in this way."

Some even sent me photos of their offspring. I asked them not to, but they carried on, flattering, cajoling, trying to convince me that they were Mr Right. But they weren't. They weren't, that is, until Charles.

THREE
A CATCH

Charles was a good-looking American of fifty-five, who had lost his wife to cancer a few years before. He had a large home in Boston but had recently moved to Turkey where his company was installing solar panels.

He sent me some lovely photos of himself. By anyone's standards, Charles was a catch. But I wasn't interested because he had a teenage daughter. He sent me a picture of her, too.

I said this to Charles, but he promised that he had an au pair and I wouldn't have to be involved. He tried to convince me what a good person he was, and we started messaging back and forth. Perhaps he was a nice guy and I wasn't being open enough, I thought. Perhaps I should give him a try...

Then we spoke on the phone. He had a soft American accent and a colourful way with words. He liked travelling and had been all across Europe. He shared my dream of seeing the world with a partner and asked if I would like to relocate someday. He was sure I would love it in Boston.

For three months, we spoke every day, for over an hour. Charles loved to chat and always made me laugh. He was convinced that our relationship would work because we had so many similar interests. We visualised all the wonderful places that we would visit together and the fun things we could do.

"I'm ready to give my all to make this work," he gushed. "I wonder where you've been all this time."

I wondered too. Why on earth had I suffered for so long when I'd found such a great guy so fast?

One day, Charles contacted me, delighted — his big work project was coming to an end. He sent me a copy of the contract, worth twelve million U.S. dollars, and the cheque he had already received for three million. I didn't ask for them; I guess he was just trying to impress me. That's men for you! I congratulated him on his success.

"Just trying to work hard," he laughed and revealed how lucky he was to land such a competitive job.

I have to admit, after three years of living alone, it was wonderful to have this regular male contact. Charles was a good listener, too. One night, he said to me, "I'm enjoying getting to know you more each day."

So was I. I felt like a teenager again, lying in the dark, listening to him.

"There was once a time when I used to lie in bed and gaze up at the ceiling," he whispered. "I wished that, one day, I would find a person who could understand me, just the way you do. You mean the world to me now."

He always texted me last thing at night. "Write me when you are up. 'Til then I will be thinking about you. Sweet dreams, my Superwoman."

Then, when I awoke, there was another message waiting. "Good morning, Sunshine. Hope you had a splendid rest. You were in my thoughts all night."

We shared our hopes. But what drew us even closer was sharing our fears — primarily, of growing old alone.

"Now you have me, let's make it happen," he declared. "Promise me you won't hurt or leave me and I promise the same, dear. Let's love each other unconditionally."

Yes, Charles started to use the L word. I hadn't heard that in a while. Of course, my husband had said it to me, but it had been meaningless. He never behaved with love. How I longed for a relationship full of kindness and trust. Perhaps with Charles I could have everything that was missing in my marriage...

But, I wasn't in love, not yet. I told Charles, how could I be in love with someone I hadn't met in person?

So, we decided that had to change. London seemed like a good place to meet because my daughter lived there, and I knew it a little. Charles agreed. He had to fly to Dublin for work then would meet me afterwards. We would spend five days in London and take it from there.

"You might extend your stay in London," he said. "I

will also check flights from London to Boston. If you wish, I would love to go with you to Paris, too."

I paid for my own ticket and hotel. That way, I didn't owe Charles anything and was free to do as I pleased. I knew this might all be crazy but if I didn't try I'd never know. Could this be the love story I'd dreamt of all my life?

By now it was mid-April. A week before the big day, Charles sent me copies of his ticket, passport and hotel reservation. He told me to dress smartly and only bring a few pairs of shoes because he was taking me shopping. London in the spring would be divine.

As he was leaving for the airport, he sent a quick text. "Can't wait to meet you. You told me you like surprises, so be prepared!"

But I never would have guessed what happened next.

FOUR

THE SURPRISE

My daughter called to see if I had met anyone, but I didn't tell her. I thought she would be worried, so I decided to wait until I got to London.

I was starting to feel very excited. This was going to be fun. Of course, I was getting nervous, too. Charles was surprised that I wanted my own hotel room, although he still booked it.

"Your wish is my command," he said. "But I'm pretty sure the other room won't be used because I want us to be together."

Charles was always polite and respectful but eventually we got on to the subject of intimacy.

"Can I ask you something?" he whispered. "When was the last time you had sex?"

The truth was, I hadn't had sex for three years. And my husband was the only man I had been with for the three decades before that. I told Charles, but he reassured me — he hadn't had sex for four years either, not since he lost his wife.

He asked about my favourite sexual position and how I liked to be touched. He revealed that he loved nice, black lingerie on women. He wanted to know if I preferred men in briefs or boxers and if I had a favourite colour.

"Don't worry, I know we will enjoy it on that special night," he sighed. "I will treat you like a queen. I want us to love and respect each other always."

He suggested that, at first, we turn off the lights. What a relief — getting naked in front of a new man in your sixties is not for the faint-hearted!

I hoped we would have good chemistry as I still hadn't seen Charles in person. We were supposed to Skype, but he had problems with his phone. He apologised and sent me pictures of the broken screen.

So, I busied myself with all the physical and mental preparations a woman makes before being with a new man. Suddenly, Charles called me from Istanbul airport. He sounded stressed. He hadn't been allowed to board the plane because he was taking his cheque for three million dollars out of the country. The Turkish government were accusing him of money laundering and demanding thirty thousand Euros in tax.

"My translator wants to get me a lawyer," he said. "I'm confused; one of the customs officers said I should just try to meet with their terms because they are very strict with foreigners. I'll wait for the lawyer, she will soon be here."

The next message came fast. "The lawyer has arrived. I'm going to remain in detention. She says that the customs and police are already involved, and I should pay the fine because a court case will end up taking even more time and money."

Charles asked me to lend him the thirty thousand. I said I didn't have it. He begged; it would just be a short loan.

"Korman construction called me," he explained.

"They will update my cheque this week. Before our trip to London, I will have fixed everything."

If I didn't have the money, could I take out a loan or borrow it from friends? If I didn't help, he would be sent to prison. He even sent me a copy of a Turkish newspaper with his photo on the front page, accusing him of being a criminal.

"Please assist me with whatever you can," he pleaded. "I'm in a tight situation. I've got just seven hours. Can't even think straight now."

So, Charles was right — he had surprised me after all. I was shocked that all the dreams and promises had come to this. Disappointment stabbed me in the heart.

He said that I was the only person he could rely on, that he had no one else in the world. Me — a stranger from a website that he had only known for three months and had never met in person!

I refused to help but still he implored. "Don't do this where there is love, Babe. I promise to pay you back with interest. Should I send you my online banking details, so you can see, dear? I still have 1.7 million dollars in there but had to freeze my account when I arrived here because my credit card was stolen, and hackers were stealing money from me."

When I insisted that I didn't want to see his account and wasn't going to give him any money, my sweet lover turned on me.

"Will you abandon me because of this? I'm surprised you are refusing. I copied all the documents for you. This is the worst thing you can do to anyone, so harsh. Is this really you I'm talking to?"

He was horrified by what a cold person I was, how I had no heart. How could I leave him there, trapped in Turkey? He became more and more angry until, finally, I blocked him.

So, the love bubble burst. I've heard stories of men cheating women for money. Now I realised that my loving, caring Charles was one of them. If that was really his name.

FIVE
QUESTIONS

I didn't fly to London. The insurance company refunded my ticket and I cancelled my hotel. I told my daughter what had happened. Like me, she was shocked.

Thankfully, a lifetime in business has given me a sensible streak and I never seriously considered sending Charles the money. As I hadn't met him, I wasn't deeply in love. He didn't break my heart and I didn't cry.

Nothing lost, I told myself. But I did feel disappointed. Most of all, that people could lie like this. I have always been very honest. Maybe too much so. That's partly why I believed my husband for so long. We always expect other people to be like ourselves.

But there it was. People cheat, it was a fact. This case was closed. I decided that, from now on, I wouldn't buy any more tickets. If somebody wanted to meet me, they would have to pay for me themselves.

Fortunately, I had other options. Charles had asked me to come off the site and stop talking to other men, which I promised to do once we had met. In the meantime, I had answered the others that messaged me. Just in case. There's that sensible streak again.

In total, I was in contact with five more men. They were like waves — some dropped off as new ones rolled in. Surely some of these must be genuine?

One of them was Ian, an attractive Californian of sixty, who had also lost his wife to cancer five years before. He came from a wealthy family but when his parents passed away, they left everything to his sister who was the eldest. But she burnt through the money on drugs and alcohol with her crazy Italian boyfriend and the family business soon went bankrupt.

Ian said that he and his sister still didn't talk. "I have forgiven her, but I guess she is still taking drugs. I'm hoping and praying that she can get clean some day."

So, after six years working in Denver, Colorado, Ian decided to strike out on his own. It had been a struggle, but the risk had paid off and now his company built roads in Dubai.

Work had taken him all over the world. He had hiked up Mt. Kilimanjaro and couldn't wait to see Everest. "But that doesn't mean I wouldn't want to travel more. I like to spoil my woman."

He was looking for a lady to grow old with, someone with a good sense of humour and open to communication. We agreed that it was best never to go to bed angry and to solve personal issues quietly and maturely like adults.

After thirty years with a man who had the emotional maturity of a toddler, this was music to my ears. Ian liked sports, films, and even dancing — when he was in the mood. So did I. He disliked liars, cheats and heartbreak. We could certainly agree on that.

He spoke of his difficulty in dating again. "Since I've become a widower, it has been hard for me. But I have made up my mind that I'm ready to start again."

I knew what he meant. To start dating at this stage in life feels all wrong — a backwards evolution from human to amoeba. But being alone forever feels worse.

Ian may have been looking for Miss Right, but he wasn't taking any chances. He wanted to know all about me. He even sent me a questionnaire.

Do you love to cook?

How often do you exercise?

Do you drink or smoke?

Some of the questions were emotional...

How do you react when you feel that you have been insulted?

Some social...

What are your political views?

Some were life's big questions...

How often do you fail people when they depend on you for help?

Others, tiny...

If the dinner is $100, how much would you tip if the service was satisfactory?

I sent off my answers but still the questions came...

What is your favorite colour, food and music?

What are the three things that you are thankful for?

Where do you see yourself in five years' time?

I felt like I was being interviewed for a job that I wasn't even sure I wanted. But still the final question made me think...

What do you miss in your life right now?

SIX

ANSWERS

WHAT DID I MISS IN MY LIFE RIGHT NOW? I missed having a man. I missed intimacy — emotional and physical. I missed love. Although Ian asked a lot of questions, he answered them too. His favourite colour was brown, he exercised twice a week, and, after a dinner that cost $100, "I can give up to $30 or $50 as a tip. You know what they say, 'Givers never lack.'"

In five years from now, he saw himself retired and exploring the world with his partner. He missed having someone to make plans with and do everything together as best friends.

Over the next two months, our virtual relationship grew. Before long we were speaking for hours a day. It seemed that his concerns were starting to fade.

"I must confess that I've really enjoyed our conversations," he said. "It has given me so much joy and courage, knowing that with faith and patience the right person will come."

His search for love hadn't been easy. "I had almost given up and thought I wasn't going to find someone that I would be able to trust and build something special with."

But the more we spoke, the more he imagined our future together. "I know we are both lonely and don't want to make a mistake, but do we know how much time we have on Earth? Since we have found someone, we should grab the opportunity because it doesn't always come so easily."

With each day, Ian's energy surged and his voice trembled with excitement. "I have never been happier in the past six years than I am now," he declared. "Thank you for doing that to me."

Then the floodgates opened. This man, once so reticent, was overcome with emotion. "I love you more than words could ever express. From the moment I saw you, I knew you were my soulmate. Since day one, we've shared something incredible, something that most people only dream of. I have been searching for you all of my life."

He became impatient to meet in person. "I feel incomplete without you and want you here NOW!"

Fortunately, his year's work in Dubai was coming to an end. "When I finish my contract here, let's take a vacation. I want you to choose the place. All expenses (shopping, boat rides, jewellery, etc.) on me. I really can't wait to get everything done and come back home to you."

I suggested we meet in London but explained my resolution not to pay for any flights myself. He reassured me. "We can stay in a nice hotel and I can get our tickets, don't worry about it."

As the big day got closer, he started to make grand promises — he would buy a house wherever I wanted and a Porsche Panamera to drive.

Ian was going to fly to London from Hong Kong. As a subcontractor to an Asian company, he had to go there with his project manager to collect his money. He sent me a copy of his cheque for $18 million and a contract. But, when he was due to leave, Ian became stressed. Apparently, he couldn't take the cheque out of the country because it was like taking out so much cash.

After my last experience, I was now starting to doubt Ian. I suggested that he ask the company to do a bank transfer. He said that they didn't like to and asked if he could send the cheque to my address. I didn't understand why and refused.

For the first time, I didn't hear from Ian for a whole day. Finally, he called. He was so happy — he had managed to solve it all and the bank transfer was done. My heart lifted. Maybe I had been wrong about Ian. Maybe he was genuine after all...

But then he called again from the airport. He couldn't leave the country without paying tax on the payment and he had no money. Could I lend him some and he would pay me back when he got to Hong Kong?

This didn't make any sense. How would they know about a bank transfer at the airport? If he had the transfer, why couldn't he pay with that? If he had now been paid, why did he need to go to Hong Kong at all?

When I refused, Ian became abusive. Again, I was called heartless and cruel. I blocked him too. Now I started to see everything in a new light. All those questions he had asked seemed less like the concerns of a nervous suitor and more like information gathering to work out how to manipulate me.

So here I was again. I guess I should have known Ian was a phony. Do you know anyone whose favourite colour is brown?

SEVEN
FIFTY SHADES OF MATTHEW

After Ian, I was feeling pretty disillusioned. Did I have the word BANK written on my forehead? Were there any genuine men on this site? I had really had enough. I was even starting to think about giving up. And I may have done... if it weren't for Matthew.

If my life were a movie, Matthew would be played by George Clooney or Richard Gere. He was a pearl, the kind of man every woman dreams about.

Matthew was a widower who lived in Monaco and developed properties. He loved art and bought pieces from auction, most recently a huge statue of a king sitting on a horse. He paid 200 000 Euros for it, but he assured me it was worth three times that.

Keen to maintain good health, Matthew got up early every day to go jogging. His family lived in London, but they often flew to Nice then he travelled to meet them by helicopter. He sent me several photos of himself with his adorable daughter and grandson.

Matthew was very good-looking, with chocolate brown hair and almond eyes. But that wasn't what drew me to him. What really got me was his voice. It was so deep and sexy, it made Barry White sound like a Munchkin!

After a brief period of messaging, Matthew started to phone me every night. I decided to play along. He told me that he had a very sexy imagination. "Me too," I laughed and sat back to enjoy the show.

He began with a disclaimer. "Well, first off, I'm no pervert or sexual predator. I respect and admire you and have all these lovely thoughts of you because of the attraction and interest between us. I hope nothing I say ever comes over as offensive to you."

I agreed that all was fine and, before long, I had my very own *Fifty Shades of Grey*.

He started gently. "I'm sure we will soon have our

own art collection. I can be a Da Vinci with a pencil when it comes to loving every part and detail of your body... But I want you to know that your dress makes me feel uncomfortable, so I'd be happy for you to take it off. All I need is you, naked, in a bed full of roses."

These images made me think of *Titanic* and *American Beauty*. Was Matthew turning to films for inspiration? Whatever it was, he soon turned up the heat.

"We will start slow and sensual with deep kissing and foreplay to make your body tickle with sensation, before I finally touch you, slow slow slow...

And then we build the speed. I want to kiss you all over until you're frustrated and finally give me your lips. Then I will bite them, tenderly, and kiss you passionately. You will never be able to get the taste of my lips out of your mouth."

Sometimes, I couldn't help but smile to hear his male ego in flight. "I will make you feel more powerful and sensual explosions than you ever felt before," he declared. "I will give you the definition of your existence. I will make love to you uncontrollably until you're exhausted and crippled."

Crippled? Not quite the right choice of word but, even so, I stayed on the line. What was he thinking about now?

"I'm thinking about how I will hold you and make love to you. I swear I won't stop until your legs are shaking and your neighbours know my name. I'm dreaming about kissing the insides of your thighs. My tongue will be like an Olympic athlete!"

I don't know if my new admirer had recently seen the 1980s film 9 1/2 *Weeks*, but he talked a lot about food.

"I will give you ice cream on a cone. I want to taste you on my fingers. I want to place cherries and strawberries on your body and bite them off, one at a time, until I get to your heaven. You're like a special pizza I've carefully ordered from heaven — so tasty!"

I did enjoy listening to all this, but I was starting to get nervous about going further and having full phone sex.

"I didn't say anything about phone sex, Love," Matthew whispered. "Of course, I want the real thing... But have you ever done it before?"

I had to admit that I hadn't. Now Matthew's voice dropped even lower. "I can stop if you want me to. I just wanted to make you feel good, that's all. Do you want me to stop?"

Well, did I?

EIGHT
ALIVE

Of course, I didn't want Matthew to stop. I was enjoying myself too much. I woke up to find "Good Morning!" texts with pictures of him still in bed, his muscular, naked torso peeking over the sheets. He asked about my dreams and told me his.

"I didn't want to wake up this morning because my dreams of us were too sensual," he said. "I can't wait to bite you, kiss your neck, pull your hair, trace your spine, hold you down and use my tongue until you're shaking uncontrollably."

What an invigorating way to start the day. Better than a cold shower!

Our discussions would last throughout the day and

roam around a wide range of subjects including golf, deep sea diving, music and art. And food, of course. He would often ask what I was eating for dinner and add, "Just be ready to be my dessert."

We spoke of serious matters too, like health and family. He had a step-sister in Norway that he had grown distant from since his parents died, which he still regretted. "Family is the only thing on earth we can't replace."

Then, one day, Matthew told me that he had a problem. I asked him what it was.

"My problem is I can't get enough of you," he said. "I can't explain how much you mean to me or why I even love you but the thing I know and can explain is that I can't live without you."

Now the conversation moved from sex to love. "I really want to grow closer to you," he whispered. "I know we have yet to meet, but my heart skips a beat when I hear from you. I feel ALIVE."

That's how I wanted to feel — alive. After so long of being closed down with my husband, unable to trust or really love, I wanted to let go. I wanted to enjoy myself fully. I wanted to live.

Matthew seemed to speak for me when he said, "My father once told me that if you live an ordinary life, all you have are ordinary stories. Right now, I just want to finish this last business project then spend the rest of my life living it to the fullest with the woman I love, doing all the things I always wanted to but felt too busy and had to postpone."

I didn't want to postpone any longer either. It seemed a shame that Matthew and I were only meeting now in the later years of our life.

"I wish we had met sooner too," he agreed. "But I'm glad you're here in my life, TODAY. I know I am not your first love but, if you give me the chance, I promise I will be your last. Soon our loneliness will fly away on the wings of time."

Okay, so sometimes he sounded like a 1980s pop ballad. Once he even told me, "I'm hopelessly falling for you like a raindrop."

But, at least, he was full of passion. "I want to swim in an ocean of blankets with you. I want to fall asleep holding your hand. I want us to ride horses and write songs and dance in the rain."

And, at least, we still had some time. "I want us to be

eighty and still in love with each other," he gushed. "I'm not the best man in the world but I promise I will care for you with all my heart like nobody has before. I want to be your harbour at the end of the day, your safe place, your friend, your lover, your champion, and, most importantly, your crazy man."

He certainly was that. But what joy to be crazy again. Maybe that's the worst part of adult life, the crippling sensibleness. The need to do the right thing and always think about the consequences.

I was tired of that too. Of course, I had doubts, but Matthew reassured me.

"There's no such thing as too good to be true," he laughed. "This is all good enough to be true because we've both been lonely and need that love and passion in our life. We deserve anything and everything we can dream about. I promise to love you forever. I told you I will make you laugh — and I will make you moan. Let's travel the world together and make love in every country we visit."

Well, how could I argue with that?

NINE
EVERY WOMAN'S DREAM

"I don't think I could live a day now without hearing from you," Matthew whispered. "I want you to know that I have never felt like this before. Ever!"

Our virtual affair was becoming intense. Matthew never held back. "If you ever leave me or break my heart, I will poison you. And then I will commit suicide because I have never felt this way about anyone."

Sometimes it felt like I was in an opera! We spoke all day then I dreamt about him at night. I became impatient for us to meet.

"Oh trust me, anything worth having is worth

waiting for," he reassured me. "This is just you exercising a bit of patience for a few weeks in return for a lifetime of happiness."

He sent me his address in Monaco and asked me to visit him there. Maybe he could meet me at the station. "Have you ever made love in a moving train?"

I told him that I wanted to meet on neutral ground, but he said I was worrying for no reason.

"I don't have any ulterior motives to manipulate you or make you fall in love with me then break your heart," he protested. "I have nothing to hide, no secrets or skeletons in the closet."

Well, actually, he had one secret that he couldn't keep any longer. He was going to buy a Rolls Royce with our initials on the seats. "And you know I'm a man of my word and I always mean what I say."

Matthew offered to meet me in London when his current project ended. He had just signed a lucrative contract with the Chinese government to develop properties in Hong Kong. But, once he got over there, he called to say that he had no cash and needed 2000 Euros to fly his lawyer out. I was surprised — why would a business like his lack a sum like that?

I refused to lend Matthew the money, so he sorted it out and apologized for asking. Of course, now I knew that he was just like the others. But I didn't block him. I wanted to see how far it would go.

Matthew didn't call anymore, he just sent messages. Next, he had to fly to Australia, where building supplies were cheaper. He sent photos of himself in Sydney, along with pictures of containers loaded with materials.

But he had changed now. He was always stressed or sick, not funny and joyful anymore. Then, as he was due to leave, he needed to pay taxes and asked me to help. When I pointed out that I wasn't a bank, he exploded.

"I can't believe what you're saying to me," he sneered. "I asked you a simple yes or no question. Why would you insult me and sell me out this cheap?"

The emotional blackmail came thick and fast. "I'm very disappointed in you. If our love ever meant anything then you would talk to me and listen instead of judging me and breaking my heart." He said that the skeptical voice in my head was not my conscience but actually my fear of love. He even asked for an apology.

Finally, I suggested that, if he needed money, why didn't he sell his statue? Now the man who a few days before had said, "I AM FOREVER FAITHFUL TO YOU...'Til death do us part" told me that I wasn't the only woman in the world and he would find his soulmate in Hong Kong.

I wished Matthew good luck, and I never heard from him again. But I didn't ever block him – his messages were far too interesting. In his parting shot, Matthew told me that, for the rest of my life, I would look for him in every man I met. I suppose, in some ways, he was right because the life he described is every woman's dream.

I don't suppose that I will ever know who Matthew really is. But I'm guessing that he has never been to Monaco, or even to the museum where that statue really is.

TEN
BIG

THIS BUMPY JOURNEY TO FIND LOVE ONLINE HAD already delivered me many new experiences. But this was another one that I didn't expect.

After just a few weeks of messaging, a man called Larry sent me a photo of his huge, erect penis. I couldn't believe my eyes! I was shocked and deleted it straight away. Later, he asked if I had received it and I told him I had erased it.

"Why?" he asked. "Look at it again. We should share everything."

Everything about Larry was big. He was a very powerful man, tall with a deep voice and broad shoulders like a rugby player. He was born in Sweden to a Swedish mother and an American father but had lived in the States since childhood. His late wife was Swedish too, but he had lost her to cancer in 2012.

Now, he was living in San Antonio. But a big character like Larry couldn't have a normal job. No, he was a gold miner. I was a bit skeptical, so Larry sent me the link to his company website, which had a big picture of him, of course. He even emailed me photos of the mines and explained the different chemicals they used.

Larry called me every day for months and our chats were always fun. He sent me happy, romantic texts so stuffed full of emojis, they looked more like messages from a teenage girl than a macho guy.

I never got to see him though, as the camera on his phone was broken. Once we were due to Skype but then we lost the signal and the image flickered off.

I wondered how it could ever work between us when we lived on opposite sides of the world, but this didn't bother Larry. A year after his wife died, he started dating again but it didn't work out. So, this time, he had decided to join the website and cast his net out wide.

Larry believed that it would work with the right person, wherever she was located. He said if we were together, we could live wherever I wanted as he had the funds to make that happen. He promised to come to see me once he finished his month-long contract in Turkey, where he was overseeing the locals working for him.

Then, one day, he sent me a picture of a big, natural diamond he had found in the mine. He had decided not to tell the Turkish government, or he would have to hand the jewel over because he only had permission to mine for gold. He instructed his workers not to tell anyone either.

He asked to send me the diamond so that he wouldn't have to pay taxes on it, but I refused. Of course, now I realised that Larry was another scammer. Who sends a diamond to a total stranger?

I decided to play along to see where it would go. Shortly after, I had another message. Now, Larry was panicked — someone had found out about the diamond and he was being taken to prison. He phoned from the police station. Apparently, he was only allowed one call and he chose me. As he spoke, a Turkish voice told him off and he shouted back, "I'm talking to my fiancée."

He even said that his "Turkish interpreter" would phone me to back up his story. A call came in from Turkey, but I didn't pick up. Larry asked why I didn't take the call, but I explained that I couldn't help him. I could hardly come to Turkey and break him out of jail.

Now, Larry got very angry with me. I didn't hear from him again for weeks. Then, out of the blue, he contacted me again.

"I didn't die in prison, even though you expected me to," he declared, melodramatic as ever.

I told him I was happy about that and asked what would happen next. He wanted to get out of Turkey as soon as possible but the government wouldn't let him leave until he paid the taxes to the tune of 50 000 Euros.

Now he asked the question I had been expecting for some time. Could I lend him the money? He could easily pay me back when he got home. He even offered to send me a copy of his bank account — he had millions in there but it was blocked because someone had tried to hack him.

Thus, it turned out that the biggest thing about Larry was the amount of bullshit he could come out with!

ELEVEN

WHAT IS LOVE?

I WAS IN THE CAR WHEN LARRY ASKED ME TO give him 50 000 Euros, so he could get out of Turkey. I had been so calm with all the other men when they asked for money and either blocked them or simply refused.

But this time, I snapped. As I was driving, I put Larry on speakerphone and started screaming, "Fuck you! How can you keep lying like this?"

My anger towards all of the men I had met online rose up in me, my outrage at the hollow promises, the deceit. I'm lucky I didn't crash. I yelled that I was fed up with his games and told him to go to hell.

Larry was upset — how could I think that he was

playing games? He tried to convince me that wasn't true. He was so disappointed that I didn't trust him. How could I put him down like this?

"I've been working all my life and I'm proud to say I'm a very successful man," he complained. "I just need a bit of help right now."

But I couldn't stop. A switch in me had flipped and I vented all my rage. Larry was shocked. I even surprised myself.

Larry claimed to be deeply offended. "Please don't insult me again because I asked for a little help. You're my last hope, that's why I asked."

But, when I still refused to pay up, he told me to go and "F" myself. I hung up. I still didn't block him though. I'm not sure why. Maybe I enjoyed our conversations too much.

Soon afterwards, Larry contacted me and apologised. We started chatting and, once again, he said lots of sweet things.

"I have to believe that God puts every single person in our lives for a reason," he cooed. "I know we will be happy when we are together."

This time I didn't get sucked back in. But, when you've been on your own for a long time, it's hard to resist the daily phone calls, the loving messages. And Larry could be very loving. But, before long, he asked for money again. I told him that I didn't have any, so he suggested I borrow some from friends.

"Don't turn your back on me," he begged. "Don't leave me here."

He said that he wasn't asking me to give him the money for free. It was a loan and he would pay me back with interest as soon as he sold the diamond.

"You have to trust me and believe in me because I will never let you down. I love you so much and I will make you happy for the rest of our lives."

When I still refused, Larry started to lecture me. "Everybody wants a stress-free relationship but sometimes things are not always smooth. That's why pastors always say in church 'for better and for worse.'"

Now the guilt trip came thick and fast. "I want a caring woman who's ready to love me for me and stand by me. She will always be there for me and never leave me or run away when I have a problem. Because I would never do that to a woman I love."

He skillfully turned everything around until I was the one at fault. "I need a woman who truly believes in partnership. She's willing to do things that she may not want to, if they are important to me, and vice versa. If you can't love and care for me like I do for you then we are not meant to be."

He told me that I needed to grow up and act like the mature woman I was. In fact, he said that I shouldn't be on the dating website at all because I didn't know anything about love.

And so, I blocked him. But I had to admit, he had hit a nerve. What is love after all? My marriage had been so full of mistrust and betrayal. My ex-husband was always telling me how much he loved me... whilst cheating and lying over and over again. Just like all these men I had met online.

Maybe Larry was right, and I didn't know what love was. But I was pretty sure it wasn't this.

TWELVE
THE SCRIPT

Larry was the last really interesting person I spoke to from the website. I met a few more guys. One was British but living in the US and had a company that mined diamonds in South Africa. He was funny and used to sing to me over the phone.

I enjoyed our chats but before long the tone changed. His machines broke down at work and the mining became slow. He couldn't meet his deadlines and the banks wouldn't give him any more loans. You can guess what happened next. He asked for money, so I blocked him.

Next was another American, an oil specialist. He sent me such long emails about love, I couldn't even read them all. Then he went to work on a project in Turkey. Now where had I heard that before?

He sent me a photo of himself in front of a very grand building. I asked where it had been taken. He said Istanbul but I recognised it as Barcelona.

When I pointed this out, he became angry. "You are a stupid woman," he sneered. "You think you know everything."

So, I blocked him too. Finally, there was an American building houses. He seemed trustworthy and kind. I wasn't so interested in him, but I went along with it to see where it would go.

He dreamt of growing old with me — another common refrain. Then he had an accident and broke his leg. He sent me a photo from the hospital with his leg up in a sling. But his insurance didn't work, nor did his credit card and he badly needed an operation. . .

Here we go again! I suggested he borrowed some money from the bank. He got it sorted but before long needed a new investor for his business or he would go bankrupt and-

By now, I'd had enough. I looked back at all the men I had met online and started to see a pattern. They were all widowers who lost their wives to cancer. They were all very religious and talked a lot about God. I'm not religious but, at the time, I thought, well, they are American!

But were they? Reading back over their messages, I saw lots of mistakes. I didn't notice them at first because English is not my first language plus predictive text can make dunces of us all.

They all claimed to be wealthy. Most promised to buy me a Porsche Panamera. But I didn't see any in person or even on camera. They all made the excuse that they didn't have a smartphone, which is unusual for a school child these days, let alone a millionaire!

Do you know anyone who has a Mercedes and a swimming pool but still uses a Nokia? Or, if they did have a camera, it was broken, and they sent me pictures of the smashed screen.

On the rare occasions they agreed to Skype, there was an image for a moment then the connection went down. Now I wonder — was a photo put up briefly then disconnected? I don't think I ever saw them actually move.

Of course, I'd like to believe I'm irresistible, but they all fell in love with me too quickly. All the questions that made them seem so interested actually helped them identify what made me tick. And the details that brought their characters to life could easily be researched online. Just put Lake Dillon, Colorado into Google and lots about sailing pops up — Ian's supposed hobby!

Perhaps the most overwhelming similarity was not one of them had a normal job, but they were all miners, property developers or road builders. After about two weeks of speaking, they also all landed a big contract somewhere abroad like Turkey, Dubai or Hong Kong.

They sent me copies of their cheques for millions of dollars — does anyone even use cheques anymore? They often sent images of their multi-million-dollar bank accounts too, which they couldn't access because someone had tried to hack them.

Next, the men went abroad to do the job but then they had a problem. They became stressed and needed money for taxes or broken machines or operations.

I started to realise that I'd been living in a romantic *Truman Show*, where nothing was what it seemed. The protestations of love, the traumatic childhood stories, the dreams — it was all an act.

These guys were so good, they should win an Oscar. But, if they were actors, was there a script? And, if so, who was writing it?

THIRTEEN
BIG BUSINESS

The numerous similarities between all my online "suitors" point to one thing — these were not one-off scammers. This was organised crime.

I wrote to the dating website to report what had happened, but they didn't reply. I wrote again and this time they just told me to change my location or age. This cold response made me wonder, was the website in on it too?

I decided to turn into a detective myself. I talked to a Nigerian friend who told me I had experienced the classic "419 scams," named after the section of the Criminal Code in Nigeria which covers fraud.

He explained that the scammers buy American or

British phone numbers, which they then redirect to Nigeria. They are usually young men aged 16-25, often living in a house together. After each call, they have a mentor who gives them feedback and advises on the moment to close the deal.

It sounded like a modern-day Fagin's gang. I asked why these charming, intelligent men didn't have good jobs. They clearly had great IT skills... and brilliant imaginations. My friend said that it is very hard to find a job in Nigeria, which is why people turn to scamming, but ironically, Nigeria's reputation for fraud stops legitimate companies investing and creating jobs.

For more answers, I turned to the origin of the problem itself — the internet. It confirmed that the vast majority of "romance scammers" are from Ghana and Nigeria, where they are dubbed "Yahoo boys" because they use Yahoo email accounts (although many now use Gmail instead).

Although these countries are fast developing, they are fraught with the postcolonial legacies of political instability, corruption and high unemployment. Almost half the ten million graduates from African universities are out of work.

The average salary in Nigeria is about $10 a day. Of course, romance fraud is hardly secure work. You could spend months wooing a mark only to find that they pay nothing — like me. For a moment, I felt guilty for wasting the poor boys' time!

I thought about how exhausting it must be, keeping up the pretense for the months required to build a credible relationship, a process known as "grooming."

I pictured the guys calling from their shared room, my name and details scribbled on a wall chart, along with all the others'. It must be so hard to remember everything. No wonder they always just called me Babe!

To create their "characters," the scammers steal a real person's photos from dating sites, Facebook or even old MySpace accounts. Sometimes thousands of phony identities are created from one set of stolen pictures. Each scammer usually has about six targets at once although one guy managed twenty-five, impersonating both men and women. He was like the Eddie Murphy of online fraud!

The "love scripts" were bought from fellow scammers or downloaded from various websites. One 55-year-old British woman was recently imprisoned for writing them. She came up with numerous heart-wrenching scenarios, including having lost a partner in 9/11. It was like she was writing a virtual soap opera.

Apparently, the scammers often liked to entice victims to perform sexual acts on a webcam, which they could then use for blackmail. They threaten to send the recordings to friends, family or employers, which they find on social media sites like Facebook. Thank God I never had phone sex with "Robert from Monaco!"

Even though there is extensive information about romance fraud online, this is a growth industry, increasing by over 30% each year. With divorce rising and families scattered around the world, loneliness is big business. In 2015, victims lost £23.3 million in the UK alone, although the true number is much higher because many feel too ashamed to report these crimes.

So where are the dating sites in all this? Many experts claim that the websites are aware of the role they play in romance fraud but often disclaim any responsibility for fake profiles. They don't warn about the dangers of internet dating for fear of putting off customers. Online dating is now worth over £225 million a year in Britain. Loneliness is big business indeed.

But it was perhaps this final statistic which struck me the most. The FBI reports that, in the US, 82% of romance fraud victims are women. And who is scammed out of the most money? Females over the age of fifty, just like me.

It feels cruel that these scammers use our ignorance about the internet against us, along with our women's emotions, like the longing for love and the willingness to help those in need.

Some romance fraud victims took it so badly they even committed suicide. But what really killed them — was it the loss of the money or the loss of love?

FOURTEEN
AN OLD STORY

When my daughter asked if I had met anyone on the site, I just said that they were all scammers. I didn't go into details. It's not nice to admit you were "catfished" — another term I hadn't even heard of before my misadventures in online dating.

But there were more surprises to come. As I researched further, I discovered that, although the internet has created these new scammers with modern terminologies, the frauds themselves are very old.

The "romance scam" is just the latest version of the so called "Advance fee" scam. We've all had those emails — a Nigerian prince wants to put two million dollars into our bank account because he can't take it out of the country. In return for transferring the funds, we can keep a high percentage ourselves.

But I was amazed to discover this scam actually dates back to the late 18th century, when it was known as the "Spanish Prisoner." A businessman would receive a letter from someone trying to smuggle a person connected to a wealthy family out of prison in Spain. The scammer promised to share the reward from the family in exchange for a small amount of cash to bribe the prison guards.

Another con, dating back to around 1830, was known as "The Letter from Jerusalem." It is surprising similar to the emails today. "Sir, you will doubtlessly be astonished to receive a letter from a person unknown to you, who is about to ask a favour..." It goes on to describe the possession of a casket containing 16,000 francs in gold and the diamonds of a late marchioness.

As email has lowered the cost of sending letters, the number of scams has risen. Some of these messages might seem ridiculous but, by sending an email believable to only the most gullible, marks unknowingly self-select. No wonder targets are known as "mugus," a slang word derived from the Yoruba for "fool."

But, like viruses, scams have to mutate to survive. Now that even the most unsophisticated internet users are wising up, scammers have found more subtle routes, like the romance scam. These appeal not just to the victim's greed but more complex emotions like empathy and the need for love.

This is an old story and one unlikely to end any time soon. I realise that I was lucky. I didn't actually lose anything — apart from a few blows to the ego and maybe the heart.

Other women's responses to being scammed varied wildly. I read about one lady who sold her house and gave all her money to her virtual suitor. Apparently, her kids were now buying her food. They couldn't give her any money as she would just give it to the scammer even though she still hadn't met him.

It's common to stay in denial like this. One guy even admitted, "I know I'm a fraudster, but I still love you." It was all his victim wanted to hear and she continued to fund him. In the most extreme cases, victims become money mules, moving cash around the world. They cease to be the victim and become the criminal. They can even go to prison themselves.

I remember a man who wanted to give me the codes to go into his account. At the time, I said no and didn't think any more of it. Now I wonder, was he trying to get me to rob from someone else's account, perhaps another woman's?

Fortunately, some ladies find ways of fighting back. One single mother from Leicester set up a Facebook group called 'Stop the US Army Dating Scam.'

Military personnel are popular for false identities because they are considered to be brave and honest — as well as looking hot in uniform! Being "deployed overseas" also provides a great cover for erratic communications and no in-person meetings.

One top US general in Afghanistan had his photos stolen and became the face of more than 700 fake profiles. He had to issue a formal statement to confirm that his wife was still very much alive, his children did not need money for any medical procedures and he *never* used any online dating sites!

One time on the dating site, I was contacted by a US military surgeon. He claimed to have killed someone in an accident and needed money to buy his way out of going to prison. I'm not sure that story evokes quite the sympathetic response he required.

However, I was touched to read about one Swedish pensioner that turned it around. At first, she was distraught to discover that the mature Danish gentleman she had fallen in love with was actually a 20-year-old Nigerian scammer.

But then she developed a friendship with the real person, went out to visit him, and now dedicates herself to overcoming poverty in Nigeria. Falling in love certainly changed her life — just not in the way she would have ever imagined.

FIFTEEN
TAKING ACTION

So, if you have been scammed, what do you do? Well, firstly, try not to feel too bad. According to a study by the British Psychological Society, sensitive people are more vulnerable to romance fraud. Don't blame yourself for being lonely or feeling empathy for someone in need.

Then try to take some action. Websites like romancescam.com ask victims to post all the information they have about the scammers like phone numbers and email addresses, along with the fake pictures and ID used.

This means that any other potential victims who are suspicious can google their suitor's name and find out the truth. It also ruins scammer's jobs and interrupts their cash flow as they have to do more work to create new profiles.

But, if you do report, don't be fooled if you receive an email pretending to be the police tracking the scammers. The same gang that did the original scam might email you from a police@gmail or yahoo.com account and promise to catch the fraudsters... then ask for more fees.

You might find that romance fraud brings out the vigilante in you. Some former victims turn "scam baiters," posing as potential targets to engage scammers in lengthy "relationships," thus lessening the time they have for real victims.

Scam baiting website 419eater.com outlines a particularly amusing case of an American identifying himself as James T Kirk then sending copies of a fake passport with Captain Kirk's photo. He was hoping that his Nigerian scammer, who had never heard of the TV series Star Trek, might use the passport in the future and get arrested.

But do scammers ever really get caught? To be honest, it is difficult, not least due to the shortage of cyber-crime laws and the lack of enforcement for existing laws, especially in African countries.

Also, as fraudaid.com explains, you may believe that you have been corresponding with one person — just as I did. But the emails may have actually come from several scammers pretending to be the same suitor.

Thus, the chances of arresting your specific scammer are very slim. However, a body of evidence may lead to an arrest warrant, which could result in catching the organized crime network to which he belongs.

At least these scams are starting to be taken more seriously. In 2004, the Nigerian government formed a commission specifically to combat crimes like Advance Fee fraud.

And justice is sometimes done. On YouTube, I saw a video of the Malaysian cell of a Nigerian romance scam gang being arrested in Kuala Lumpur's airport.

Perhaps the rotund middle-aged man in handcuffs was my loving Charles from Boston, my sensitive Ian from Colorado, or even my sexy Robert from Monaco. Or their brilliantly manipulative mentor. I will never know.

So, what now? I had been in contact with about twenty scammers in total, albeit some of them very briefly. I have to admit that, overall, I enjoyed the conversations with them, even though I never knew who they really were.

Sometimes I even found myself missing them. I might think of something that would make Charles laugh or infuriate Ian and want to tell them... but then I remembered that they weren't real.

Of course, I was lucky. Apart from the six-month subscription to the dating site, I hadn't lost any money. I could put it down to experience, an adventure on my hero's journey.

But it was time to climb out of this rabbit hole for good. I thought about what to do and eventually decided that, although I had been bruised, I wasn't beaten. My quest for love wasn't over. Not quite...

So, I joined another dating site, this one run by a British newspaper. A colleague of mine had friends who had met their partners on there, so I knew it had at least some real people.

I redid my profile and uploaded my pictures, this time without my daughter's help. I wasn't frightened anymore. But I had become cynical. Now, when someone wanted to befriend me, I had two questions... Where do you live and what you do?

If they said that they dug oil, mined for gold or were military surgeons, I blocked them straight away. I had started to learn how to walk the winding path that runs through this mysterious, virtual world...

SIXTEEN
A NEW IMAGE

I would like to say that after I joined the new UK site, I was inundated with genuine requests. Sadly, that wasn't the case. I never would have thought that the questions, "What do you do?" or "Where do you live?" were so challenging. But, in this shadowy cyber world, they cut to the chase.

In fact, now I was asking these questions straight off, lots of men were deleting me. Were the romance scammers sharing my details with their colleagues and telling them that I was a waste of time? Was their mentor warning them about me?

I still occasionally got messages from oil miners or property magnates or military personnel. But when I asked if I could see them on camera, they all had broken phones. If I pushed the issue, I never heard from them again.

Unfortunately, the few real guys that did get in touch, didn't attract me. When I asked one what he did for a living, he said that he stacked shelves in a supermarket. I was surprised — he was an educated person, why didn't he find something else? But he explained that he just didn't want the responsibility. Hardly Prince Charming stuff!

Could I ever really love a man who would say such a thing? Maybe my expectations were too high. I knew one had to compromise in love and, at my time in life, I couldn't expect a Brad Pitt to sweep me off my feet. But when is a relationship a healthy compromise and when is it giving up?

I just didn't know anymore. I started to feel like the more I communicated with men, the less I understood what they were looking for.

Another man from the new site contacted me, who had a job and even a working camera phone. He wasn't exactly my dream but at least he seemed normal — which, in the bizarre realm of internet dating, is a huge compliment!

Even better, he soon got onto the subject of meeting in person. I said that I was in London that week and suggested we have coffee.

"I don't do coffee," he replied. "But I have spaghetti and a bottle of wine at home if you want to come over. It's up to you."

No, a bowl of pasta wasn't enough to tempt me to go around to a complete stranger's home. I was shocked by his arrogant assumption that it would be. Does this technique really work with any women?

Finally, one rather nice man liked me on the site. I asked him my usual questions, but he replied that, although he liked my profile, I lived too far away. I was a little annoyed and asked if he was looking for someone who lived next door. He confirmed that yes, he wanted somebody nearby.

It seemed strange to me as I was looking for the best partner possible — wherever he might be. Of course, it would be handy if he was in my neighbourhood, but should you really choose your lover by their postcode?

So, the first real possibility vanished into thin air. Then, as he hung up, something caught my eye.

When Larry the gold miner turned out to be yet another scammer, I had blocked him on WhatsApp. But he hadn't blocked me, so I could still see his messages. And now I saw that he had changed his photo.

Whereas before he was a big, strong white man of about my age, now he was a good looking, young Arab guy, with deep brown eyes, wistfully staring out the window of his car. Quite a makeover! I considered if this picture was any more real than the last or if it was just more appropriate for his latest target.

And what was he called now, I wondered. Larry didn't seem to fit this new image. Perhaps he had gone for something sexier like Omar or Aziz. But, of course, I will never know.

SEVENTEEN

THE FINAL STRAW

I WAS EXHAUSTED WITH THE DATING GAME AND close to giving up. At my daughter's insistence, I downloaded Tinder and created a profile. But I couldn't bring myself to swipe through the guys on there. It seemed too much like flicking through the Argos catalogue. You might choose a new fridge like this but surely not a mate?

Now and again, I glanced over my profile on the UK dating site. One man my own age had liked me, so I liked him back. I clicked onto his profile and read that he lived in the town where my son was working. So, I sent him a message to tell him and he asked to chat on WhatsApp.

But when he sent me his phone number, I noticed

that it had a German area code not a UK one. The first sign that something was off. My antenna was finely attuned now.

When I enquired, he said this was because he was currently in Syria but had to use different codes. He couldn't use his business phone because he was working for the Secret Service. But, of course, he couldn't write that in his profile. So now I was talking to James Bond!

Apparently, he was retiring soon, and his contract would be finished in a few weeks. Now where had I heard that before...

His wife was dead from cancer and he had no family. I asked him to Skype, but he had an old phone that didn't have a camera. That sounded familiar too. He sent me a photo instead.

"Come with a camera and you will see me alive," I texted.

"Why are you asking so many questions?" he replied and sent me another picture.

When I explained that I merely wanted to see him in person, he got angry and told me that I didn't have an open heart. I said I was sorry and wished him luck in finding the right person with an open heart. Then he blocked me.

I received one more message from another man my age. His photo was taken from so far away, I couldn't see what he looked like, but he refused to send more images, declaring that he wanted to meet first. He didn't even want to chat before we met because he valued his time.

As I was visiting my daughter in London, we arranged to meet. I suggested having a coffee but again he refused. As it took him an hour to get there, he at least wanted to have lunch — he valued his time.

I decided to be polite and agreed. While I went to meet him, my daughter did some shopping. As she walked away, she even reminded me, "Be nice!"

So, I entered the restaurant and asked if there was somebody waiting for me. I was directed to a man sitting there but I was shocked. He looked twenty years older than me, at least.

I'm not looks obsessed, but this seemed a bit much. The meal was okay, but he drank several glasses of wine and revealed that he usually got through a whole bottle every day. My ex-husband was an alcoholic, so this was a red flag for me. When my daughter met me afterwards, she whispered that he looked even older than her grandfather.

This clearly wasn't my match. So that night, I decided to look at Tinder. It had picked up all the men in London and I had seven hundred likes.

Perhaps I should have been flattered but I just felt tired. I no longer had the strength to communicate with them all and find out if they were real people or just scammers. I had a quick look at the photos, but I knew that I couldn't trust my eyes anymore.

It was the final straw. I deleted my online profiles. I had lost all hope of finding my partner there.

But there was one more man that kept contacting me. My ex-husband. He was crying, sorry for everything that he had done. Now he understood what he had lost and couldn't live without me. He begged me to start again.

I felt so confused. What should I do? Could I really go back? Was this the only option for me now?

EIGHTEEN
THE OLD WAY

It was all getting too much. I just felt so emotional. I didn't know what I wanted or expected from relationships any more.

My ex-husband phoned every day, crying and begging me to start again. He claimed that he wanted only me. He longed to hold me and kiss me, just to be with me and grow old together.

"Why now?" I asked. "Why didn't you want it years ago?"

I wanted him to explain why he brought other women to our home. Just so I could understand. What was the problem? Was I not attractive enough? Was it me? But he didn't want to talk about it. He just said that he needed to check that he could still "be a man."

I told my ex that I didn't trust him. But, for some reason, I didn't say that he would never have a chance with me if he changed. Perhaps I was too scared to finally cut the tie. Yet all this upset me even more. I didn't want to go back. I longed to move forward. I was still looking for the right person. Surely, he was out there somewhere?

I now felt that there was very little chance for me to meet my man on the dating sites. It was hard work to keep searching and messaging. Even if I lived in London, having to meet up with all those men on Tinder would drive me crazy in the end.

But I also believed that we should never give up on our dreams and I had decided to enjoy my life with the best partner ever. I couldn't turn back now.

I told my Nigerian friend about my struggle. He lamented the difficulty of modern dating and noted how, in traditional African society, the Auntie would have helped.

This wasn't necessarily a blood relative but an older lady in the village who found the best matches for you. But these days, local communities have broken down and people barely know their neighbours. There is no longer that person who knows all the singles in the area, who could identify who belonged with who.

"Sometimes the old way is the best," he said and smiled.

I wasn't sure if that was true. But, not long afterwards, another friend told me about a private matchmaker. Apparently, he interviewed you then would hand-pick men that he thought you might connect with — for a price.

My friend gave me the matchmaker's number, but I put it to one side. I wasn't sure about it; it seemed so old-fashioned. Then I discovered that professional matchmaking is actually a rising trend. So many people have become frustrated with the cyber search for love, they are choosing this method instead.

The professional matchmaker is a once-noble, long-standing profession. It was a feature of societies all over the world that had arranged marriages. In traditional Japanese culture, they were known as the

Nakodo. In Chinese culture there is even a goddess of matchmakers called Nu Gua.

Some cultures maintain the custom — today, 55% of marriages globally are arranged. In these places, many families still hire an intermediary who knows a large variety of eligible young people so can make a match that satisfies both sides.

However, these matches are usually more about the size of a bride's dowry and reinforcing strong family connections than any affection the couple shares.

Yet some claim it's a better option. In a recent study, the global divorce rate for arranged marriages was only six percent. Compare that to the divorce rate of "love" marriages, currently around 42% in the UK.

One of oldest practices of professional matchmaking is in the Jewish communities of Eastern Europe and Russia. There, the woman known as the "Shadkhan" was crucial because many of the villages were so isolated.

This tradition is famously portrayed in the musical "Fiddler on the Roof," when the young woman sings,

"Matchmaker, Matchmaker,

Make me a match,

Find me a find,

Catch me a catch…"

I used to love that film. I started to sing the tune to myself as I picked up the matchmaker's number.

"Matchmaker, Matchmaker,

Look through your book,

And make me a perfect match…"

Have things really changed so much since then? Regardless, if I was to continue with my quest, I needed a new strategy. So, I put my doubts to one side and made the call.

NINETEEN
THE MATCHMAKER

I ARRANGED TO MEET THE MATCHMAKER WHEN I was next in London. I felt reinvigorated by the thought of receiving professional help with my search for love.

I waited in the designated place, an exclusive bar in the West End. But when the matchmaker arrived, he was not what I imagined. Here was a smart, professional man in his late forties, who looked more like a lawyer than a matchmaker. What was I expecting — an old crone in a headscarf, carrying a basket of bagels?

We had a glass of wine and began the interview. Well, I knew that's what it was, but it just felt like a friendly chat. He asked me lots of questions about my likes and habits, even how often I'd ideally have sex.

He was so smooth and discreet that I didn't even realise he was taking notes. He was lovely and seemed quite a catch himself — although I sensed that he wouldn't have been interested in any of his female clients!

The matchmaker described how he would introduce me to three potential partners. All the gentlemen's details would be thoroughly checked, including their backgrounds, health conditions, financial status, and if they had any criminal issues or other potential skeletons in the closet. It felt like I was hiring a private dick!

At the end of our hour together, he smiled and asked, "Do you want to go ahead?"

All I had to do was sign the agreement, approve my profile, which he would personally create, and then, of course, pay. Now there's the rub — this service wasn't cheap. Dating apps are either free or about the cost of a monthly subscription to the gym. But for the price of this exclusive matchmaking service, I could have bought a car!

I wasn't sure what to do. I have worked hard all my life to ensure a comfortable pension. Yes, I could dip into my savings, but it seemed so indulgent. And, of course, it could be a complete waste of money and yield no results.

But I didn't feel like I had any other choices. I was so afraid of being lonely and dying alone. Was this my last chance to find someone? Could I really put a price on that?

So, I agreed and shook his hand. After a couple of weeks, he sent me the first two matches to see if I wanted to have lunch with them. I was giddy with excitement but, when I read the men's profiles, they were both 75 years old!

I had told the matchmaker that I would prefer a man up to the age of 65 — he asked if I could go to 67 but we never mentioned above 70. At that age, would there really be enough time left to enjoy life to the fullest?

Having looked after my useless cheat of a husband for thirty years, I did not want to commit to caring for an old man for the rest of my days. I am still young in my heart and soul.

Truthfully, I wanted someone my own age. But the men all wanted a woman that was ten years younger — at least. It seemed cruel. Perhaps this was understandable at an earlier age, when men may be driven, consciously or unconsciously, by the biological urge to have children. But by now, it seemed like hypocrisy on their part. Didn't these guys look in the mirror at all?

Despite my reservations, I decided to give them a chance. So, I went to meet the first man, a widow of 75 with no children. Our meeting was nice enough, but it transpired that he hadn't actually paid a fee to join the matchmaking service because he couldn't afford it. So much for those thorough financial checks!

After lunch, the man asked me to be friends on Facebook. I agreed and was polite but when I told the matchmaker that there was no spark between us, the gentleman had already beaten me to it.

I went to meet my next date. At least, he was my age — but he was also my height. He was a smart guy, who knew lots about wine and drove a Ferrari. But, when I asked why he had divorced, he admitted that he had cheated on his wife and showed no remorse. He didn't ask anything about me at all.

When I enquired what he was looking for, he replied, "Nothing." It turns out that the matchmaker had contacted him on Linked-in and asked him to meet me. He wasn't even looking for a relationship.

Finally, the third date cancelled before I arrived. He was also 75 years old and he had a panic attack on his way there! I was devastated. I felt like such a fool. I had resisted all of the scammers online only to fall into this shiny-looking trap. How could I have wasted my hard-earned cash on this?

I just made it back to my hotel, before I burst into tears. But, once I started crying, I couldn't stop. The tears flowed — for my failed marriage, the years of betrayal and heartbreak, and all the disappointments through this dating experience. It started so promisingly but had turned into a nightmare.

I cried until I was exhausted and fell asleep. In the morning, I got up and prepared for my flight home that evening. Suddenly, my phone pinged with a message. What fresh hell was this?

TWENTY
AWAKENING

I looked at my phone. I had a notification from Tinder, the one dating app I hadn't deleted. Tinder shows your location so, because I was in London, I received a like from a man who was nearby. Well, it wouldn't hurt to look at his profile, I thought.

His name was Adrian and he was a retired restaurant manager. He was a widower, whose wife died of a heart attack two years ago. He was sixty-six years old but in very good shape and had a full head of hair.

I sighed, what did I have to lose? So, I liked him back. Then he answered me straight away and asked if we could speak on the phone. I agreed, so he rang me on

FaceTime, coming on camera from the first. How unlike all those men from the dating sites.

We chatted for a while and it turned out that we shared at least one true passion — golf. He wanted to meet but I told him I was leaving London that night. Adrian wasn't available that afternoon because he had a golf tournament. But when I revealed that I lived abroad, he cried, "Ok, I'll come now."

So, we met in a café for a few hours. I immediately took to Adrian, with his mischevious sense of humour and his warm eyes. He wasn't wealthy and didn't drive a sports car, but he was sensitive and kind. Perhaps those are the true riches in life...

When I got home, Adrian called me every day and we got to know each other more. As the weeks passed, we found we could talk about anything. If I didn't like something or had a contradictory opinion, I would say so, and he would listen. No subject was out of bounds.

Straight away, I felt relaxed. Instead of making sure I did my make-up or held the camera phone to show my best angle, I didn't care how I looked. I could be myself. He always complimented me too, which made me feel good.

At first, Adrian didn't know where my home country was – he had to Google it. But after a few weeks, he came to visit me there. I didn't tell my daughter. I felt very nervous — he was staying for ten days, which is a long time when relations are strained.

But I shouldn't have worried. The connection between us shone and we had such fun visiting the city's museums and parks. He cleaned my car, joking that I needed a man around for these jobs. We even played golf together — the first time I had ever played golf with a date!

At the end of his trip, Adrian went home but the phone calls continued. The next month, I went to stay at his house in England. This time I told my daughter. She was worried and put a tracker on my phone. How she would have protested if I had ever done that to her!

When I landed in London, Adrian met me at the airport and whisked me away. We spent a wonderful week together in the warm summer's sun. He took me on a boat trip down the Thames and to an outdoors classical music concert. Nobody had ever treated me like this before. It was the most romantic week of my life.

In recent years, I had been spending time and travelling only with other women. Now I was out, holding hands with a man, one who was taking care of me, making breakfast, driving me around.

I had to admit it was exciting. It had been so long since the last time I was close to my ex-husband like this. This man woke a feminine emotion inside me. I felt crazy, like I was twenty years old. He put on music full blast and we sang along at the top of our voices. He offered to teach me Rumba dancing. He even called me 'Babes!'

And he was very sensual. Amazingly so. I had never experienced anything like it before. It made me happy to realise that life was not over for me in this way. I had worried that I might be celibate forever, but he made me see that there was hope.

Now autumn is coming and the trees in the park are turning brown. But Adrian and I are still seeing one another, flying back and forth across the seas. In some strange way, it feels like destiny that we met. I went to London to see the matchmaker's contacts that weren't interested in me and ended up meeting Adrian instead.

I know it is early days and we will see what life brings. But I am happy to have the chance to spend time with a kind, sensitive man who spreads positive energy wherever he goes. When we wake up, he smiles and says, "Morning, Babes! How are you today?"

Of course, I don't know if it will be forever. But, for now, I have decided to enjoy the moment. "Go with the flow," as my daughter says.

I have discussed this with Adrian and he agrees that, the minute we don't enjoy it anymore, we will stop. We are at the age when we shouldn't do things we don't love. But each positive emotion we give and receive in life is a gift. This time is ours.

AFTERWORD

Returning to dating in my later years was a strange experience, like visiting a foreign land. The world has changed dramatically since my youth, most noticeably with the development of the internet. These days, food, clothes, and pretty much everything imaginable can be found online without even leaving the house. So too with the search for love.

Online dating is becoming increasingly normal as the way of meeting people. Yet, when I first joined dating sites, I felt totally unprepared for what was to come. Like many women my age, I had no idea what was really happening on these sites or how many scammers were on there, fishing for the right catch.

As I experienced most of the main patterns in

"romance fraud," I wanted to share them so that other women would not be fooled in the future. My advice to any woman doing internet dating is to stay grounded and find out who people really are before you get emotionally attached. Don't let sweet-talk carry you away from reality into fantasy, no matter how charming the man or how desperate your need for love.

Social media is a new phenomenon people of my generation often struggle to understand. Nowadays, when I am sitting in a café, I see couples sitting opposite one another, playing with their phones.

Perhaps it is easier to chat online than face-to-face and to type your feelings rather than looking into another's eyes and speaking aloud. It may seem alien at times, but this is a new world and we need to adapt accordingly. There is no going back.

Life is supposed to be fun and miracles can happen at any age. Although the modern world can be bewildering, we are lucky to live in a time where a woman can reinvent herself in her sixties and beyond. It doesn't have to just be knitting and a blue rinse from here on in. We can create a life for ourselves that fits the age we feel rather than the date on our birth certificate.

Ultimately, my adventures in dating in my later years helped me to fall in love again, not least with life itself. Yes, the search for Mr Right can be tough at times but keep going! Never give up your dreams and take each new experience as a lesson from which you can learn.

Despite all the challenges, I am very grateful for this exciting adventure, which opened my eyes in so many ways. As well as meeting another, it has helped me find myself.

ABOUT THE AUTHORS

Audrey Lindt

Audrey is over 60 and divorced after 30 years of marriage. She worked hard her whole life, becoming a CEO and managing over 500 employees, whilst raising her children at the same time.

Until the last few years, she was so busy that her personal life was not a priority. She didn't have time to give it much thought. But when her children left home, she lost her motivation to work. She decided to reduce her professional duties and concentrate on her hobbies to fill the emptiness inside.

Audrey has been always healthy and young at heart. When she was young, her biggest dream was to see the world. But when she reached the period of life when she could enjoy it fully, she found herself alone.

Her marriage had been a great disappointment and

she had never experienced a healthy relationship with a man. She longed to enjoy the best that life had to offer with a partner by her side, so she set out on the search to find a soulmate online.

Twitter Audrey Lindt Author

Facebook Misadventures In Mature Dating

Jacqueline Haigh

Jacqueline holds a BA in English Language and Literature from the University of Oxford and an MA in Scriptwriting from the University of London. She has over fifteen years' experience as a writer, working for all platforms including film, TV, online, stage, radio and books.

The Elder, the short film Jacqueline wrote and directed, premiered at the Monaco International Film Festival, winning an acting award for its star, and Jacqueline wrote, directed and presented *Do You Come Here Often?* a comic documentary about reincarnation for Channel Four.

Jacqueline teaches writing and works extensively in story development. She has script edited hundreds of screenplays in all genres and has developed, edited and written several books for The London Ghost-writing Company.

Jacqueline also performs stand-up comedy on the London circuit and appears in comic storytelling shows at festivals worldwide.

www.jacquelinehaigh.com

Twitter @ JacHaigh

Made in the USA
Las Vegas, NV
03 January 2022

40167183R00069